"This is an arresting first book; it gives us a poetry deep in particular moments and eloquently alert to the world's curious and agitated detail. Alan Michael Parker's poems are full, as poems should be, of surprises which turn out to be simply true."

—Richard Wilbur

"Notions of the casual, the consequent, the conditional—so many poems here start 'If . . . ,'" "How . . . ,'" "Because . . ."—preoccupy this mindful poet, who may be otherwise characterized by invoking three nouns which as proper names become totems of our contemporary poetics: bishop, justice, strand. But mere identification of overtones, even of undertones, will not suffice: Parker's autonomous qualities are: *clarify, fervor, glee;* these are the new notes sounded—no, rung!"

—Richard Howard

"With *Days Like Prose,* Parker has written a poetry of living music and sonic complexities, whose textures modulate from the circumspect to the resplendent. Whether meditating on the Sears catalogue or narrating a widow's recent grief, these poems intimate rather than explicate; they bespeak the reticence in the folds of the world."

—Alice Fulton

"In this marvelous debut collection we discover an eloquence so humble that at first we may not recognize its profound and sometimes dazzling elegance. These are poems in which the formal intelligence often touches true wisdom. *Days Like Prose* is a masterful accomplishment.

—David St. John

Days Like Prose

Days
Like Prose

ALAN MICHAEL PARKER

WordFarm
SEATTLE, WASHINGTON

WordFarm
334 Lakeside Ave S, #207
Seattle, WA 98144
www.wordfarm.net
info@wordfarm.net

USA ISBN-13: 978-1-60226-019-1
USA ISBN-10: 1-60226-019-2
Printed in the United States of America
Cover Design: Andrew Craft
Second Edition: 2019

Library of Congress Cataloguing-in-Publication Data
Names: Parker, Alan Michael, 1961- author.
Title: Days like prose / Alan Michael Parker.
Description: Second edition. | Seattle, Washington : Word-
Farm, [2019]
Identifiers: LCCN 2018055906| ISBN 9781602260191
(pbk.) | ISBN 1602260192 (pbk.)
Classification: LCC PS3566.A674738 D39 2019 | DDC
811/.54--dc23
LC record available at https://lccn.loc.gov/2018055906

P 10 9 8 7 6 5 4 3 2 1
Y 24 23 22 21 20 19

For my parents, Donald Parker, and the late Ellen Parker

CONTENTS

ACKNOWLEDGMENTS

Antaeus: "Tsankawi"

Boulevard: "Landscape with Cows"

Grand Street: "Gents'," "Lullaby," "Epithalamium: In Our Cities"

The New Criterion: "Two Suns," "If Steam Is Water's Memory"

The New Republic: "A Little Something," "Song," "Up," "7 Types of Congruity," "Hopscotch"

The New Yorker: "Alchemy"

The Paris Review: "Days Like Prose," "Hush," "The Meniscus," "The Ticket," "The Sears Catalog"

Pink: "The Fence," "Above the Timberline"

Raritan: "The Geese"

Shenandoah: "Facts and Figures," "A Short History of Numbers"

TriQuarterly: "The Widow," "Magpie"

Western Humanities Review: "The Copper Beech," "Reading *Antony and Cleopatra* Aloud on Summer Vacation"

"Mud" appeared in *The Forgotten Language: Contemporary Poets and Nature* (Peregrine Smith, 1991).

"Gents'" was also included in *The XY Files: Poems on the Male Experience* (Sherman Asher Publishing, 1997).

In "7 Types of Congruity," Section II contains a quotation from Fujiwara Teika, *"Hana mo momiji mo/Nakarikeri,"* as translated by Earl Miner (*An Introduction to Japanese Court Poetry,* p. 13.)

With thanks to the New Jersey State Arts Council, for a grant that aided in the writing of this collection.

With thanks, this round, to Felicia van Bork, Eve Mitchell, and Davidson College.

PREFACE TO THE 2019 EDITION

HELLO, OLD FRIENDS. What a delight to reconnect, in some cases thirty years later, and to see what we've become.

In rereading these poems—some of which were written while I was a graduate student in the 1980s at Columbia, others over the decade that followed—I have felt a little dizzy, time itself the subtext. Here are ideas I have been writing and rewriting all of my career; here, too, lie promises I am keeping only today. The young poet's influences seem on the surface in this work, a first book necessarily indebted to the writer's betters. And so, yes, in my ear, I can hear Richard Howard's witty, pointed commentary on the ending of one poem, and the verb he so kindly proffered as a present for another. (Of course, *my dear,* one accepts.) Here, too, I remember with fond horror Joseph Brodsky's comment when he first read published work of mine—"Okay," he said, nodding at the page, from him a compliment, as I stood in the presence of that astonishing mind and tried not to cry. I was on my way.

Thankfully, however, the vertiginous work of rereading these poems resists the pangs of nostalgia. In rereading these poems, I have come to see nostalgia as the poet's bane, not only for the emotional harm inflicted by nostalgia upon seeing, but also for the debilitating sadness incurred by valorizing one's own past. Retrospection—I remember, I was there, this *was*—I can process, even when beset by memories. Nostalgia, no thanks. Nonetheless, precursors abound, the germinating of philosophical problems I continue to engage, not to mention the first appearance of my favorite family of imagined neighbors, the Saunders, who have appeared in almost every book I have written since, poetry or fiction.

I am struck by the ways poetry has changed. These poems

were written on papyrus—or so it feels, now—and xeroxed, handed out to friends, mailed with the hope that the return envelope would not be needed, that the Important Editor would want to keep a poem or two for publication in a journal with a circulation approaching 500. These poems might as well have been *samizdat,* for all of their reach. Before the onslaught of image-driven media, the Internet, the cell phone; before a couple of Bushes, an Obama, and a Trump, the poems here seem almost pre-Lapsarian in their innocence (although what the latest Fall would be, I could only opine). Suburban, urban, literary, personal, elegiac, formal, political, social . . . all of these terms would apply differently to poems written today. *Days Like Prose* reads from another century, because it is, even though I hope the poems are neither dated nor outdated (see how those words mean so similarly; how time makes of language an antagonist).

Some provenance: *Days Like Prose* is my first published collection, written and revised from the late 1980s until eventual publication in 1997. During those years the manuscript was submitted to various contests, as well as solicited by presses and editors, and named a finalist twenty-five times—including runner-up at Carnegie Mellon University Press, Northeastern University Press, and the Yale Series of Younger Poets (accompanied by a nice note from James Dickey)—until Andy McCord at Alef Books published the volume in his first-book, letterpress series. A book of poems! *Days Like Prose* validated externally my years of writing, rewriting, reading, and study; and rereading it still feels good.

I am fortunate to have the support of readers and editors, with this new home for old friends. With my gratitude to Andy McCord at Alef Books, for first welcoming my work into the world. I remain thankful, too, to Alice Fulton, Richard Howard, and David St. John for their wonderful blurbs; and to the late Richard Wilbur, to whom I sent the manuscript as a cold call, barely knowing the man but loving his poems, and who responded with an astonishing endorsement. Such generosity of spirit remains my ideal—one met by the fabulous Crafts at WordFarm, for their interest in re-upping *Days Like Prose*.

Alan Michael Parker
January 1, 2019

A LITTLE SOMETHING

Because a doe broke through the Saunders' fence
to starve beside the heated pool, her thin
ribs cupped like fingers leaking light. Again,
the kettle whistles, dogs bark—and the sense
we make of being singularly *here*
evaporates. The kitchen window steams
as anywhere, from any steam; the same
fruit ripens on a sill: four brown Bosc pears.

Out of the whirlwind, orange pekoe tea.
Dull marigolds offend the telephone.
Against the din—a faucet drips, a grown
man shies from God—the day ends quietly.

Because the tea bag dangles in its noose:
a cul-de-sac, a house, a pet excuse.

DAYS LIKE PROSE

Epistemology, and all the afternoon
clouds perform their dying, tusks and trunks
dissolving in a rivulet of cold wind,

the sky a promise darkening.
Will it rain? The rain says it will
as thunder pools in every vowel,

beading in the wild raspberry patch.
Epistemology, and through the sliding
glass door of the moment,

here is what I think: a man loves
being loved, shirtless on the lawn,
singing the song of a fat life,

of giddy children trampling the lavender.
I close his eyes as the red darkness
blooms inside, the sky recurring

just so—and deeper in the night
when the planes come out to fly,
their windows clean with dreams,

and the dead heroes jostle
in too-brilliant tombs, I shall sleep
the cool sleep of the unexamined,

and I shall pray the dizzying wheel
might spin again. Epistemology,
the evening mist sprawls in the grass,

the happy, roaring dandelions
bow with dew. Here, I plan
to give up planning, watch the seagulls

dive for shiners in the foam—
where the neap tide unravels as
a warning buoy bobs beyond the known.

MUD

A blur of elements, a cataract
of sod—the canyon sloughs its juniper
and sagebrush with a shrug. High-tension wires
snap: blue sparks sizzle to the ridge and back.

Beyond the barn, the Dodge, the ambulance
and fire truck; past the flush of volunteers,
cheese sandwiches and coffee, sacraments
of natural disaster, slumps the owner.

He'll rise. He'll take his slicker from the fence
and join the wake, his house and pond and shed—
goddamnit his tomatoes—choked with mud.
And still he thinks: *There are no accidents.*

His property, his body. All that is
or will be mud, and loss, and artifice.

SONG

And the walls came tumbling down.
And the word for wall
came tumbling down.
And the dust came to mean
that which has tumbled.

She ran from the city, her
hands afire. And
where she touched
she burned. And the word
for fire came burning.

The smoke rose.
And the word for sky
became the word for smoke.
She plunged her hands
into the river. And she

burned the water. And
the water burned the banks
on either side. And
the word for burning
spread to the fields.

In the fields the wheat
burned, and came tumbling
down, and rising up
went the smell of bread.
And the word for bread

became the word for clouds.
And the word for tumbling

down became Jericho,
Jericho. Jericho
came tumbling down.

GENTS'

In the Gents' room between acts
at the Regional Theatre, talk is corn and beans,
the drought not a lack but a thing out there.
We're all in line to go: one guy asks
after his neighbor's chickens, prices at the yard,
but clips conversation to fix
his stare to the wall. It's something
not to see, his body posted and tightened
into privacy, gone invisible. Like how
the houses here grow their windbreaks:
a quiet thicket of blue spruce in the middle
of a field, and no one will ever
notice us, hiding in the open.

An usher goes by, ringing in Act Two.
Sooey, says a voice in a stall, and all
the gents laugh. It's a revival,
the seats harder than remembered,
cushions for rent for 50¢ and everybody pays,
joking about the tax man. And the lights
go down, the other play resumes:
the gents sit up in their bodies,
scattered about the house, waiting for rain.

LANDSCAPE WITH COWS

Time is but a gate between the fields
of *non* and *sense,* a self-
made fence to keep us
in our lives, which I would leap
to know your mind—
as summer tolls *I told you so.*

Mountains score the sky.
They might as well be ideas
in the distance, monuments to time
which thin the air to nonsense.
(I would climb.)

Near the stream, cows ruminate.
They are cows. Moved
by happenstance, they sit, they eat.

Patience is a dragonfly, purple
and impossible as
reason. (Here's a reason:
I pretend to be
a man acting like a boy.)

I would know your mind,
alight between the fields,
balance like a dragonfly.

I would dip my wings
in what is yours and what is mine.

TWO SUNS

Like a slap
            the second sun
arrives, arranged
            as though all errant
images were imprisoned
            in its image.
Pane by pane
            the Pan Am building
fills with flame,
            south from 50th.
Why not!
            The world is wholly
all its worlds,
            alibi and alias,
and *black* contains,
            bemusedly, its *blueberry;*
why can't a cantilevered
            thought include
the fact of a mirage,
            a mirrored moment
in the sun's
            second sun?
It can. It does.
            It fills two
buckets full, brimming
            with each breath—
and winter, and *will,*
            and a long walk
down Park, downtown,
            doubled with light.

THE WIDOW

I

She remembers how the pain
took the form of an afternoon walk:
past the mill wheezing with sawdust,
through the pulpy tang of scrub oak

and wild lilies by the water,
where all she knew seemed as slick
as the creek's four stepping stones.
There was the willow: there she sat

on the burled roots, almost
somewhere, in between.
This made her late, so she hurried
back to the house, her hands

knotted into fists, gripping her skirt
as she ran, the memory of a fist
gathered on each thigh. Did she think,
then, as she swung wide the screen door,

that any day might be different?
She cannot remember when this thought
became hers, all those times together
smooth as custard. Or like milk

in tea—yes, she remembers thinking
the day seemed like milk in tea.
Her living room was dark. No one
looked up from the curve

of the sofa, sleepily, unseeing.
She expected no one, imagined
no one, but thought all the same
her words might meet with more

than their own emptiness, or the afternoon,
corporeal with dust. There she hesitated,
neither from loneliness nor want
but to sip a long sip of the possible;

there she saddened until she became
her own ruin in the evening,
flickering about the kitchen
and in the glimmer of the bedside lamp,

falling softly across the pillow
as she eased into a comfortable
early bed, falling on the letter
she had intended to write.

II

Stunned by too much television—
sprawled in the attic, in the dry rain
of fiberglass insulation; raw as memory,
which may be a kind of loss

when one will not forget—
she topples the piles of magazines,
flattens the city of magazines,
the years of *National Geographic*

reduced to a simpler time. Someday
she would have to do something

with all this stuff, all these pages
of maps that refuse to be tamed;

the Sea of Tranquility, the nerves of the eye.
Some other day. For now
what she wanted were the photos,
boxed and beribboned, captioned

in ash-gray, her Instamatic shots
of a puppy skittering on linoleum,
goofy for a knotted sock. *What was
that awful dog's name?*

she asks the ceiling fan, the air
tightening. *Am I dead?*
Someone's white dress rustles.
Her hand throbs as from a deep cut.

III

*Name a ten-letter word for
"covered with small scales,"*
he had commanded her, oh,
she can't remember when.

There were his blue eyes swimming
one to a lens, and the newspaper
dipped in blueberry jam. There were
the slippers she had tried

to throw out. *Sorrow
is the loss of sound,* she thinks,
thinking of his coffee mug—and then
of her father visiting her sickroom,

the drawn blinds pulsing like a vein;
the carpet mined with lemon drops,
used Kleenex, and the overturned
gray flowers of a jigsaw puzzle.

There he had sat at the edge of
her fever, reading aloud
the market news. "Squamulose,"
she tells the butter dish

this morning, having looked up
the word and found other words:
spurtle, sprit, and *sprink,* more
meaning than she knows

how to make. It feels like living
inside a doll, moving a doll's hands.
It feels like the summer she was
condemned to summer camp,

writing home to tell her parents
that she had died. And, oh, what a look
her father had given her, on Visiting Day—
the look she learned to want

from a man, as though through water,
the look he gives
when making love, the look
that quickens as it dies.

UP

Morning snow and even the cars look pretty.
Even the telephone wires, even the electric transformer
mounted behind the Saunders' shed,
the gray metal box filigreed with sleet.
Even yesterday's ice, still asleep.

From the kitchen radio the usual news
perks like coffee—updates and commercials,
the slush of rush hour—until the anchorwoman
drops her almond croissant
as the traffic copter hits a blinding squall
and is forced down into the storm.
Russ, are you there? Russ? Russ?
Furious rotors whipping, the clangor
of metal shearing, visibility
reduced to the altimeter's spin—

and beneath the huge whirling machine
a student stands in the pith of the snow,
wrapped in sweats on the tennis court,
practicing his *t'ai chi ch'uan.*

What he must have seen!
From the steady, ancient balance
of fingertip, wrist, and elbow,
through the shoulder with a constant, precise
dripping of water, all his weight
pooled in the arch of the right foot . . .

with an idea of marble, with a marble eye
he looked up into the falling light.

To be clapped by the roar of being.
To look up, to open a fist
slowly, uncurling each finger until
the palm cups the soul, offers up the soul.

He looked up into everything
there was, and then he stepped
away, perfectly.

HUSH

The kosher bakery on Friday morning
fills its orders with a prayer—the long,
lean baker's fingers braiding challah,
kneading loaves of fleshy, sour rye
into that extra inch the appetite
knows better than to take. There
two counterwomen smile and bicker,
aprons stained and yet unspotted
by sweet flour, sweet failure,
a daughter married off, a son gone bad.
Hush. The picture window fogs with smell
as all the pretense of the world I want
glistens, redolent with circumstance;
as all the Heavens were a Bell.

WHEAT

Believing in signs, walking the gravel road
through fields of wheat and light,
where a thought is the shortest distance
between two trees, but getting there
might take all day. The land is complete
horizon, and everything that happens
may be seen for miles:
the sun, the clouds, the lack of rain;
the question that came between us
like a fist (I looked down,
you licked your lips).

A car goes by;
wave to the car.
A child wakes in the backseat:
Are we here?
Yes and no.

Believing in a means,
the car in its dust, the distance
between a woman and a man,
a body in motion, still in motion.

It's too long a walk to town
just for bread and the paper.
(Will you be there when I get back?)
At the general store Mrs. Williams
asks the youngest Marcus,
Mm. Is that a popsicle?
And the radio says to a telephone,
Hello, hello. You're on the air.
And inside of me
it pours, and the fields drink deeply.

THE FENCE

for David Craig Austin, 1961 - 1991

Purple with dying, two words sit on a fence,
two little people, waving.
Watch them closely, see the one

lift the serif of a brow, uncurl a thin smile,
prepare to ease the other's last momentous

hop down into the cool, dewy grass,
grass cool as a forehead.
Loss is what one word might give

to the other, saying, *Here, have this.*
They look away—are they anxious?

They swing the little legs of their letters.
What could that word be waiting for,
where would he possibly go

if a breeze just strong enough,
barely stirring the black birch tree,

were to pick him up, catch him up,
wear him down to a whisper
in the inchoate sun? He is

only a word, he has nowhere to go
but home, where he is, welcome home.

SONG AS IF THE SPIRIT WORLD WERE FLESH

Let us exchange the *here* for *there,*
the clock for the hour, the starling
shivering on the wire
for the blood she tries to hide inside,

the you for I. Let the atom be
its bomb, the junkyard dog its bark.
I would hurry through your smile,
hungry for the light it makes:

let us trade the sugar for the cake.
Between the world and its demise
we lie, knot and string, I would do
most anything to know the reason

wearing eggplant-purple
makes you cry, I would trade
the sadness for its eye.
Far from here a highway overpass

cannot be seen, a rumbling line of fumes
against some other sky. Trucks clack and drone
their shifting, jostled freight
in the dead Latin that is commerce,

all cart becoming horse.
Should the mind be
manifest, the spirit world flesh,
a truck could turn into its streets,

a night into a windowpane,
a trucker into getting there again.
(Oh, if you were mine, then mine
would be its prayer, my *here* your *there*.)

LULLABY

Sleep and rain, two gangsters.
The day lined up, a murder of crows
on a telephone wire and still
the current runs. I would sleep
but dream of waking; rise
to walk the feed-corn field,
lashed by wind, stalk and silk
leaning as if to listen.
Listen. Sleep and rain,
two moles. Nose to nose
in the city of the mad plumber,
where each has the right of way.
Tomorrow's in the trees, an air-
brawl of starlings, a riot of leaves,
the sun in its music box where it sings
to itself. Sleep and rain,
two ladies in a hat store. And home
to tea in the library, to read
the novel of each other's palm
and dress for dinner. Night
steeps in the flower vase, succulent
in the lilac's hundred fists.
Sleep and rain, two dancers on a cliff.
I would sleep but for the rain.

MAGPIE

I

So terrible a scold above the squat adobe,
the borrowed house and bed, the preposterous
bulimic cats. Ugly bird on the roof
above the blue Mexican water glass

rocking on the rickety nightstand.
Magpie, clamor and kin, the world lolls
upended, for the woman I love
is sad, and showering again.

II

Cut into a mesa sits the little soul's hut:
little table, plastic plate, bag lunch,
and Sunday's news. Where possession of
the good takes a form of beauty,

and the hermit who can bend the light
around his shimmering hand
sleeps in a chair. Magpie, stubborn
as a muse, where do you hide?

III

Particle and wave, ball and chain,
the body tethered to the body.
A magpie flies in the empty, crooked
palace of the sky, as everything

falls west with everything we say,
sliding into hieroglyph
sidelong as a coachwhip snake,
sibilant and obsolete.

IV

Of appetite, and what I know
cannot be mine. Of indiscriminance.
Of the magpie on the roof, who will eat
what there is, and in whose call

our lives are satirized.
The woman I love dries her hair,
leaning into a towel, persistent
as a wish, in this borrowed house.

ABOVE THE TIMBERLINE

The impossible truth: I asked God
for a pair of gloves
and there they were, proving
nothing. In the immense emptiness.
The horizon in my head.

We need new rules. Waiter,
some new rules please.
I clap my hands
and the air claps back.

Life is furious. Thin breath
whistles in my chest.
The body knows another language
altogether; we embarrass each other
with our own ideas.

There are no trees here,
nothing against the sky.
I believe
but I don't know how.

THE MENISCUS

Wild asters. A blue
wasp shudders in the gravel.
Laundry on the line:
yesterday, the day before.
Lie down, to where
the crickets leap,
where an ant shoulders
a mountainous crumb—as the sun
fills the jungle grass, sifting
through three o'clock. There
are different kinds of hours
to spend: some harden
like a fossil, some peel away to
emptiness, some burst
on the vine. There are
different kinds of memories.

Do the fingertips remember?
The elbow seems to know
what the infant likes.
The blood hums to the moon's tug.
Reflex is a memory,
a muscle in a sleeve,
while sleep is soon forgotten—
and breakfast, and making
love, aside from
the last time we made love.

There are memories like olives,
clinging to a pit: anger,
fear, each electric
childhood shock. There are

memories like air,
the dream-scrawl of cumulus,
the man I'm sure I've met.

Four o'clock. An hour
spills into the next.
I've met this man before,
this abstract, crooked man.
Softly, my future spends his day.

IF STEAM IS WATER'S MEMORY

The given: sumac, iris, summer rain,
and sparkling asphalt steam on Lighthouse Lane.
A shirtless hardhat swigs a beer, reclines
beside a DANGER: PEOPLE WORKING sign.
Why here? This is the place where echoes go
to die, where history's brisk undertow
deposits mussel, horseshoe crab, and whelk:
the ocean roaring in a fist of chalk.

If steam is water's memory, then mist
reclaims a continent submerged—iris
and ditch digger adrift in sleepy beds;
the sumac swamped by thick Atlantic weeds.

If A, then B. The street recounts its Rome;
the hands recall their clay, the mind its moon.

7 TYPES OF CONGRUITY

I

In a biplane over Anchorage,
the white snow roaring
in its quiet knowledge
                                    like the roar
        of plankton, the roar of the giraffe
        in the half-chewed trees,
the roar of the mouse-tail
in the mouth of the python,
        the sizzling roar along
        the filament in a bulb;
the roar of the sea, not
in a shell but in a Styrofoam cup,
        among people, surrounded by people;
the white snow roaring
like her skin.

II

Fujiwara asks, *What need
is there for cherry flowers
or crimson leaves?*

What need can there be
but desire?

III

Her hair is neither
like straw nor flax. It is not
like tinsel, or the wire tendril
of a plastic plant.

It is not like the rain, or
a twist of light by Vermeer.

IV

. . . as a bay grows fishermen
Or hills a shepherd . . .

so the body grows its heart.

V

I learned about her knee today,
its stingy way of bending so, right
at the bone, where least expected.
Never have I known the rules of thumb
and elbow as comment on the future,
the possibility of what's beyond
a bend: in the shepherd's crook
or the hinge of black tsunami,
like butter folded into dough.
I learned about her knee today,
the very angle of her laugh.

VI

small talk
trumpet and snare

a parade in the wrists, streamers

her tired hands thin
blue as dusk

and the blood's steady tuba

VII

The moon pleads with the parking meter,
the postman's shoes with the basement window,
the newspaper with the fish it wraps.

On a corner, in a stairwell, look—
no one's watching, please.

Crimson leaves, Fujiwara,
her body is crimson leaves
in a wind-swirl of lies.

FACTS AND FIGURES

I end this night with Exhibit A:
the moon on the roof but it won't be long.
Now Miss Rose, our neighbor, takes
her shower in the wall.
The sound means *light,* before the day goes off.

What to buy: a prayer shawl, a teacup,
a bag of flour, tuna fish.

Exhibit B: the garbage truck is an elephant,
a lumbering rogue sneaked into town.
An elephant and Egypt and
when I die I will be buried
at the dump, entombed among
the things I couldn't use.

A houseplant, maybe even a cyclamen?
A wood chisel, three-quarter inch.
Apples for pie.

Ladies and Gentlemen, dear souls,
Exhibit C: the crooked man.
My left leg works, my right limps;
my foot is a wild dog.
I have no glorious wrinkles;
my hands are my best ideas.
My hands are my only ideas.

Apples for pie. A teacup.
Do without the houseplant.
A prayer shawl.

HOPSCOTCH

I

Beautiful and useless,
borne by the mailman, God
in safari mufti; stamped and metered,
sorted for delivery. He trudges up
the brick stoop steps, three, four,
brown knees flashing, white socks
falling. What a day,
what a job, what
a way to make the living
feel alive, the circulars and flyers,
discounted come-ons, the dumb
hum of now, urgency's ink.
An afternoon ripped open,
torn at the corner,
shaken fluttering to the floor.
(Tomorrow sealed in another
envelope, late to arrive,
nearly over when it does.)

II

Sun tea and a sprig of mint.
The inevitable ruin of ice.
A calendar divided, ruled by weeks,
tacked to the month's waterfall.
Dear Occupant, Dear Resident,
dear anybody home.

III

Beautiful, yes.
The hopscotch of hours, chalk tossed on ahead.
A chorus, a can-
can, a plague of aluminum
mailboxes kicking up a heel;
the red flag stuck
in semaphore, *something for you*
or *nothing today.*

IV

A dark V of sweat spreads
across his shoulder blades, shirt
rippling with vertebrae,
sinew, and strain—
and striped by the blue
strap of his carryall,
a cotton diagonal. His back
looks like a flag, or a country in motion,
flexing its map. (Oh, the long,
dry sentence of an afternoon.)
There he goes, across
the street, climbing
the neighbor's walk, stairs, porch,
five, six, screened from the vicious
barking of the self
left alone.

THE TICKET

Pulled over, parked, indicted by the high
beams flashing in her rearview mirror, pure
as loss, the car refracted to a blur,
she shuts her eyes and climbs in, down the spine's
white rungs to where there are no crimes but love.
A pool of water. Sumac, cypress, elm.
The perfect ease of fish in perfect tombs.
She hugs her knees, her sky, her soul's small proof
it is—and then, *Yes, Officer,* she feels
her mouth apologize. *I know, I was . . .*
She climbs back up the ladder to the phrase
marinating in its alcohol.
Yes, Officer, I know. I was, I know.
But oh, God, I can't make myself slow down.

THE GEESE

October. The sky is cool
and ripe. All day the light
thins to a filigree:
skein of geese, leaf,
cold stream. This is
a fine time, the year
in a jeweler's glass.

Two ideas: I will be
more like the world,
or less. More would mean
smaller measures of success,
each moment as a ripple
on the sharp surface of a pond:
a brown trout nods
and preens, gnats swarm
in a last daze, a frog
flabbergasts himself.
There I am in each;
vain, docile, and afraid—
but ready to forget the single
act, as I act.

Less like the world,
the man rakes his leaves,
a sum of himself.
Up above, a sycamore
scrawls its scrimshaw
in the wind, erased by wind;
balloons from the high
school football game
soar to a speck. Less

like the world, I am
captain of this glass
body, sailing. And if
I break before I wake . . .

Don't forget the geese,
the cloud commands the house.
And the house shudders
in its gutters and drains.
I am less like the geese,
more or less like the world;
a ripple on a pond,
captain of the day.

THE COPPER BEECH

for A. M.

Puritan old soul, the copper beech seems absolutely
mystified with starlings, with the cumulative
clicking of dirty yellow beaks,
the splendor of iridescence,

and the jerky, mortal nervousness
birds share. From afar, from the wicker
ease of sun tea and a heavy blanket, the afternoon
Globe and its discontents, one can imagine

the tree as a kind of thought
fulminating in a busy skull—
or high on its ramparts as an ancient city,
a fortified Troy rankled into war,

the perpetual whirring of war.
And there stands the same Hector, always
younger than remembered,
the city beyond his dying arms.

He could do no more.
And when all was lost, even then
the Greeks would take his infant son,
to be certain in death

there could be no vengeance.
Patroclus, Hector, Achilles, Astyanax.
The killing and the killed,
the body dragged and the dust conjured.

But here, in the brilliant
astonishment of starlings, flushed,
numinous, panicked into air—
for what reason!—and in the remaining

ruin of the tree, of Hector and his
bloodied hands; here in this skull
that is always the same
front porch and wicker rocker, copper beech

and distant sorrow, something else . . .
A door opens, a dog barks,
a light flickers on and on it stays.

TSANKAWI

Instead of knowing, learning. How a place
becomes an absence, sand and rock defined
by what is gone. Or petroglyphs in lime,
torn open: fish nerves, spirals, snakes, and lace
eternities. How we imagine *soul*.
Where silence fills itself, a vowel dreamed
by Plato—shattered by a sudden mule-
deer's panic, crashing through the boreal green.

For privacy is worship's better half:
we find ourselves alone entirely
among erosion's rust anemones
and mica elephants upon a shelf.

In faith, the desert's ocean, stroke by stroke:
a crawl, a butterfly, a dead man's float.

EPITHALAMIUM: IN OUR CITIES

I

What is the word for kitchen
in your country? What

are the words for long hallways
cool as water? Where

did you spend your childhood,
listening through what closed door?

The peaches on your table,
are they as fleshy and adamant

in how they clutch their stones
as the peaches here, as

my heart is? What
is your word for heart?

II

The used car lot is a metaphor
for nothing. Windshields

are not eyes, or wheels legs.
Nothing moves, but when it does

it moves in short straight lines.
We do not move like this, no matter

how we may want to,
not even when walking

in our cities. We do not
make love like this, or cry.

And our nights are darker;
and what we want of another

world is never a choice
of things. Come to think of it:

engines are not metaphors,
or roads, or even cities.

In this used car lot
little stands between us.

III

From pasture to peach orchard,
the cowbells ring their dusk-canticles

and the fruit trees hum a wind-hymn.
The air is white.

What is a prayer, if not
this moment? I carry

my thoughts to you in my hands:
peaches, and I am

a tree, will never be
as tall and wide and full again.

Forget knowledge. I know
so much less than

the faith of the orchard,
cowbells, and a peach on the branch.

IV

Your sixteenth year was a Japanese garden;
mine was a long hallway.

My first kiss was a tin can;
yours a medieval etching.

Meeting you was a walk
in an olive grove, heavy sacking

spread beneath the trees.
Meeting me was different:

also a walk in an olive grove,
but a dog barking somewhere.

V

I want to eat in your kitchen,
to see where you sleep,

to watch you sleep.
I want to see you rest

your cheek against your hand.
I want you to drink

slowly from a tall glass
because I feel like glass;

I feel like cool water.
There are places in your house

that I want to be shown,
to catch sight of myself.

VI

This is a tour of the puppet factory:
these are the insides of trees.

This machine is responsible
for the space between your eyes;

this machine produces facts:
distance, and the measured open gaze.

Here we have parts for a girl puppet,
and similar parts for a boy.

Here we have the distance
that keeps them apart.

Here is the machine
to make the holes in puppets:

this is a pile of shavings;
it is also a pile of holes.

In this last room the puppets
are tested. They dance

on our hands like children
or little gods. And the boy puppet

waves to the girl puppet
over the roar of machines.

VII

Words, you say, are glass
so each one must reflect

its origin. On the end
table: a cup of water.

And the cup is to the water
what sand must be to the common

lap of the ocean,
wanting and holding; cousins

by function and in light.
Tell me again what words are

so that I may sit in the easy chair
in the sun's violet hour.

What is your word for cup?
What is your word for water?

You are not like any water;
water is like you.

LACRIMAE RERUM

How your letter set me thinking,
letting go of words for thoughts
the way the Saunders' maple drops

its feathered ton of burnished leaves:
one good frost becomes the strange

memento I pick up on my morning walk
and carry midair, lug on home.
It made me picture our acquaintance, a poet

dead two years, a man you know
I never liked, his soul beset

by walking, drink, and form:
fourteen steps from porch to shed,
another bourbon gone down wrong.

Where he is now there are
no words but nouns, no verbs

to move us through our lives.
And there your letter made me go,
the sole unquiet thing. I took

along my son, now six months old,
and took a longer walk. I thought

of you, your wife, this awkward
curling leaf, and hoped for everyone
your boy comes home.

THE SEARS CATALOG

Because somebody's father bought a house
sided in aluminum, blue as a robin's egg,
and lived in it through two wars, buying

plaid shirts and steel-toed boots, day and night
a shot and a beer. Because, as Emerson says,

*the only thing grief has taught me is to know
how shallow it is.* Because the pages always
curl with use as though they were burning slowly.

Because you can go to town or stay at home
and your kids can go to town or stay at home

and their kids. Because the women in their bras
peek through the window of a boy's adolescence, giggling.
Because, and it's Emerson again, *Souls never touch*

their objects. Because somebody's father
lives in a blue house but can't make himself care

for doing the lawn, for edging, for raking leaves
curbside, piling the coins of a lost Empire.
Because the sky has its suburbs, its planned

communities and empty public plazas,
its strip malls gray with buckled sidewalks;

and the sky, too, has its heavy book,
fat with the glossy photos of someone else's dream,
blistering, sulphurous with what must come.

ALCHEMY

On the first good day of yard work
winter pours from my body,
soaks my shirt with its brine.

Out of storage, window screens fleck the lawn
like great farms seen from the air.
My fingers wriggle in new work gloves,
itching to do a little digging, to join
the earthworm's long, dark translation of the world.

On the stoop by the porch, a locust has left
a carapace intact, a good idea of himself.
In his kingdom, what's done
in the name of introspection
can often be a curse.

A lone toad hops on into town, passes Big Man,
knocks back a gnat, and goes underground.

Here for a moment, mine
is a small lot: I only
turn the soil, and often
fail to recognize what I uncover.

In light of the crocuses,
in their still-blooms,
the garden begins as
a patch of dirt:
anything can happen.

READING *ANTONY AND CLEOPATRA* ALOUD ON SUMMER VACATION

The yellow tractor's complicated mind
Thinks nothing of its driveshaft, thresher, screw,
Or baler, autonomic steel; as spewed
Chaff caps a pickup truck, the engine whines

For oil. Two seagulls peck in febrile dirt,
Two saucy birds triumphant, rapt with food.
They think of nothing; nothing thinks. The good
Fat little worm serves up its own desserts.

For now and never, you and I. Across
The lawn, embalmed in dusk, our tiny deck
Takes shape, a dais built to resurrect
An ancient sorrow, nailed against the house. . . .

A field hand waves. We wave. His radio's
Pneumatic heavy metal drills the wall,
The sky. One boy, two thousand years, and all
Time scorns all love, in Nile, Ontario.

A SHORT HISTORY
OF NUMBERS

The thick-skinned pterosaur,
the saber-toothed tiger, the dodo
fat with obsolescence.
I could count to ten like this,
every number hollow as zero.
We're the only species to clear
our throats before we
say I love you.

I love you.
We're the only species to pray.
The woolly mastodon, the cave bear
with skirt-thin hips.
It's a January night.
We're the only species to make
clothes to sleep in. This is
a prayer. I love you.

The platypus, the cockatrice,
the Irish elk with antlers wide
as a sunset. It's snowing:
sleep well. I love you.
We're the only species with numbers
to tell us when to sleep
in the clothes we made,
when to pray, when
to clear our throats,
what to say.

The tiny ammonite, the plated

stegosaurus with backsails
to regulate body temperature.
It's snowing: the city vanishes.
We're the only species to cry
when happy. I'm counting
to ten to remember I'm happy.
I love you.
Eight, nine, ten.

ABOUT THE AUTHOR

ALAN MICHAEL PARKER is a novelist, poet, essayist, and cultural critic. He has written and lectured widely—including at the Sorbonne and on the Menominee reservation in Wisconsin—on subjects ranging from the history of beach house art to casinos that sell Matisse paintings. The author or editor of seventeen books, including *Whale Man, The Ladder,* and *Christmas in July,* he has received numerous awards, including three Pushcart Prizes, two inclusions in *Best American Poetry,* the North Carolina Book Award, two Randall Jarrell Poetry prizes, the Fineline Award, the Brockman-Campbell Award, and the Lucille Medwick Memorial Award from the Poetry Society of America. His poems have appeared in *Antaeus, Boulevard, The New Republic, The New Yorker, The Paris Review, TriQuarterly,* and many other journals. He is Douglas C. Houchens Professor of English at Davidson College, and he also teaches in the low-residency M.F.A. program at the University of Tampa.

OTHER BOOKS BY ALAN MICHAEL PARKER

POETRY:

The Age of Discovery (Tupelo Press, forthcoming, 2020)

The Ladder (Tupelo Press, 2016)

Long Division (Tupelo Press, 2012)

Ten Days, ten poems, with ten drawings by Herb Jackson
    (Origami Lake Press, 2011)

Elephants & Butterflies (BOA Editions, 2008)

A Peal of Sonnets, seven poems, with book artist Zachary
    Carlsen (Gendun Editions, 2006)

Love Song with Motor Vehicles (BOA Editions, 2003)

The Vandals (BOA Editions, 1999)

Days Like Prose (Alef Books, 1997)

NOVELS:

Christmas in July (Dzanc Books, 2018)

The Committee on Town Happiness (Dzanc Books, 2014)

Whale Man (WordFarm, 2011)

Cry Uncle (University Press of Mississippi, 2005)

EDITED AND COEDITED VOLUMES:

The Manifesto Project, with Rebecca Hazelton (The University
    of Akron Press, 2017)

Intimacy, with Debra Kaufman, Richard Krawiec, and
    Stephanie Levin (Jacar Press, 2015)

The Imaginary Poets (Tupelo Press, 2005)

Who's Who in 20th-Century World Poetry, Editor for North
    America, with Mark Willhardt (Routledge Books, 2001)

The Routledge Anthology of Cross-Gendered Verse, with Mark
    Willhardt (Routledge Books, 1996)